ALPHABET POCKET

Written by Linda Milliken
Design by Wendy Loreen
Illustrated by Barb Lorseyedi
Cover Illustration by Patty McCloskey

CONTENTS

© 1994 **Edupress** • P.O. Box 883 • Dana Point, CA 92629

ISBN 1-56472-019-5

TEACHER'S GUIDE

Alphabet Pockets provide a fun-filled, interactive way to enhance and reinforce alphabet and beginning reading skills. Integrated with your classroom curriculum, alphabet pockets and the alphabet-related pictures can effectively:

- *Develop letter recognition*
- *Reinforce beginning letter sounds*
- *Build vocabulary*
- *Teach categorization*
- *Enhance memory development*
- *Increase object identification*
- *Develop small motor skills*
- *Integratate with bilingual instruction*
- *Merge with literature*
- *Promote spelling skills*

All instructions and patterns for making the pockets follow on pages 4-5.

The accompanying alphabet pictures can be reproduced, front and back, colored and cut into classroom sets for cooperative activities. Pictures can also be reproduced for each child to complete as letters and sight words are introduced.

Here are suggested games and activities that will implement alphabet pockets and pictures into your curriculum in a variety of imaginative, meaningful ways.

PERSONAL POCKETS
Make a pocket for each child labeled with their name instead of a letter. Use personal and/or classroom picture sets.

Hide and Seek
Hide several sets of pictures around the classroom. Ask children to wear their pocket and hunt for a specific letter represented by a picture. When found, the child puts the picture in their pocket.

Pick a Picture
Give each child several pictures to put in their pocket. Have them select one to hold up and identify either by beginning sound or word identification.

Picture Match
Hold up the word side of a picture and ask the children to find the matching picture to put in their pocket. Ask children to say the word in a second language to integrate into bilingual instruction.

© Edupress   *Alphabet Pocket Fun*

26 POCKET PARADE

Have children make a pocket and picture set for each letter of the alphabet as the letter and/or sound is introduced. Children will become adept at pocket making as the weeks progress.

Pick Your Pocket

Wear a letter pocket filled with the corresponding pictures. Ask children to retrieve a certain picture and identify it by letter sound and name.

Stuff a Pocket

Ask the children to look for pictures in magazines or coloring books of other things that begin with letter or sound being reinforced. Have them cut out the pictures and "stuff" them into their pockets. This can be a take-home activity that involves parents in a fun-filled learning activity with their child.

CLASSROOM POCKETS

Make a set of pockets to hang on the classroom wall or place in a center.

Letter Pass

Pass out a set of pictures so that each child has several. When a letter or its sound is called, the child with the corresponding picture puts it in the correct pocket.

Mystery Object

Fill the pockets with a surprise object that begins with that letter. Ask them, "What is the mystery object in the "K" pocket?" Give a clue. Ask a student to reach in the pocket and pull out a KEY! Encourage students to bring a mystery item to put in the pocket of their choice—no valuables, please!

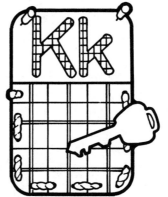
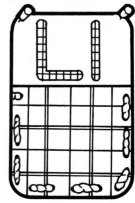

CLASSROOM DECOR

Look and learn with interactive pocket displays!

Wall Chart

Paste a corresponding picture on the front of the pocket along with the block letter for an inexpensive alphabet chart.

Bulletin Board

Put words or letters on a bulletin board. Put pictures in several pockets. Provide pushpins. Pull out a picture and match it to the letter or word. Leave intact until all pictures have been matched. Take it apart and start over again!

POCKET ASSEMBLY

1. Trace (or reproduce) pocket front and back onto construction paper.

2. Match the front to the back. Punch holes on the dots, going through both pattern pieces.

3. Stitch the pieces together with colorful yarn. Tie yarn ends with large knots. Pockets may be stapled together, if preferred.

4. To wear, punch two holes at the top of the pocket back. Cut yarn long enough to hang from the shoulder or around the neck. Thread an end through each hole. Tie a knot to hold in place.

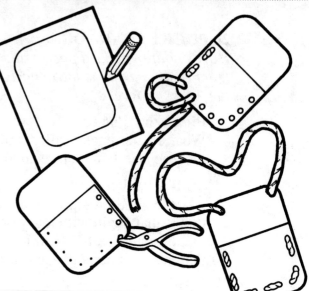

TIPS:

• Laminate the pocket pieces before stitching or stapling. Clear laminating film can be used for the pocket front enabling children to see the pictures inside.

• Use wallpaper samples or gift wrap to create "designer" pockets. For example, use paper illustrated with planes for the "P" pocket.

Alphabet Pocket Fun

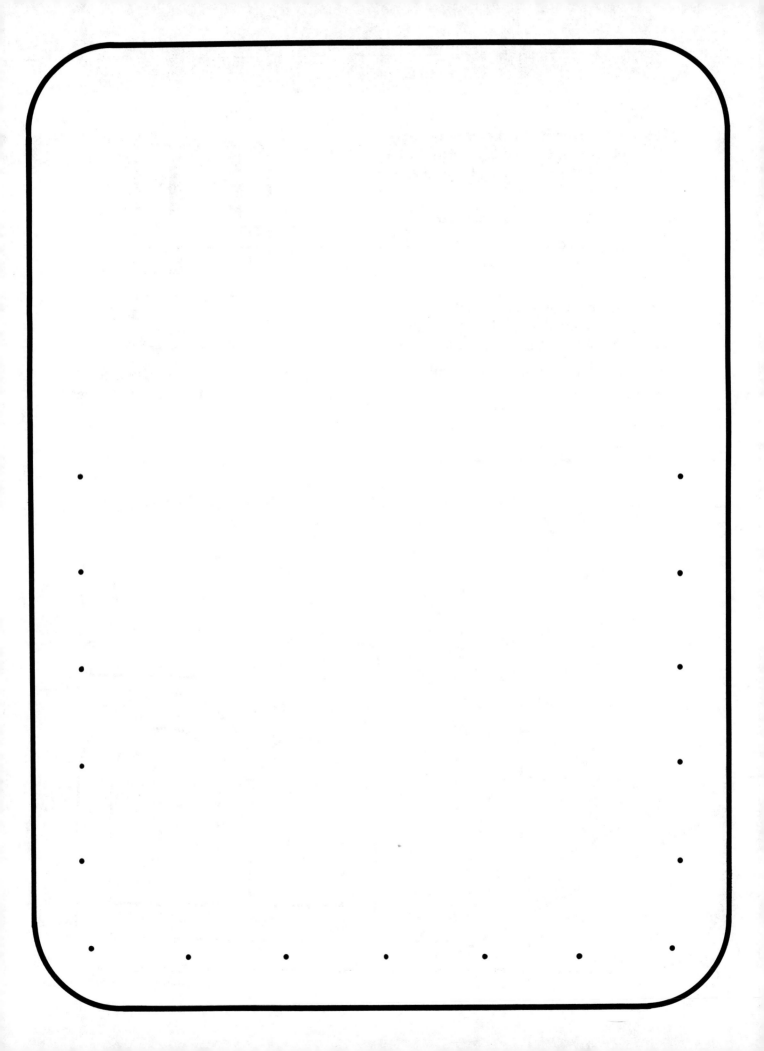

Alphabet letter patterns are provided on the following pages. Use these patterns for the creation of letter pockets, alphabet charts and bulletin board displays.

There are several ways to use the patterns.

- Cut and trace tagboard letters to create sturdier patterns for classroom activities and pocket sets.

- Reproduce, color and cut letters from lightweight bond, giftwrap or construction paper for classroom pocket sets and decor.

- Reproduce a letter set for each child to color and cut for individual pockets.

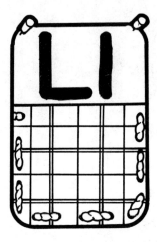

Paste upper and lower case letters to pockets as shown in illustration.

Alphabet Pocket Fun

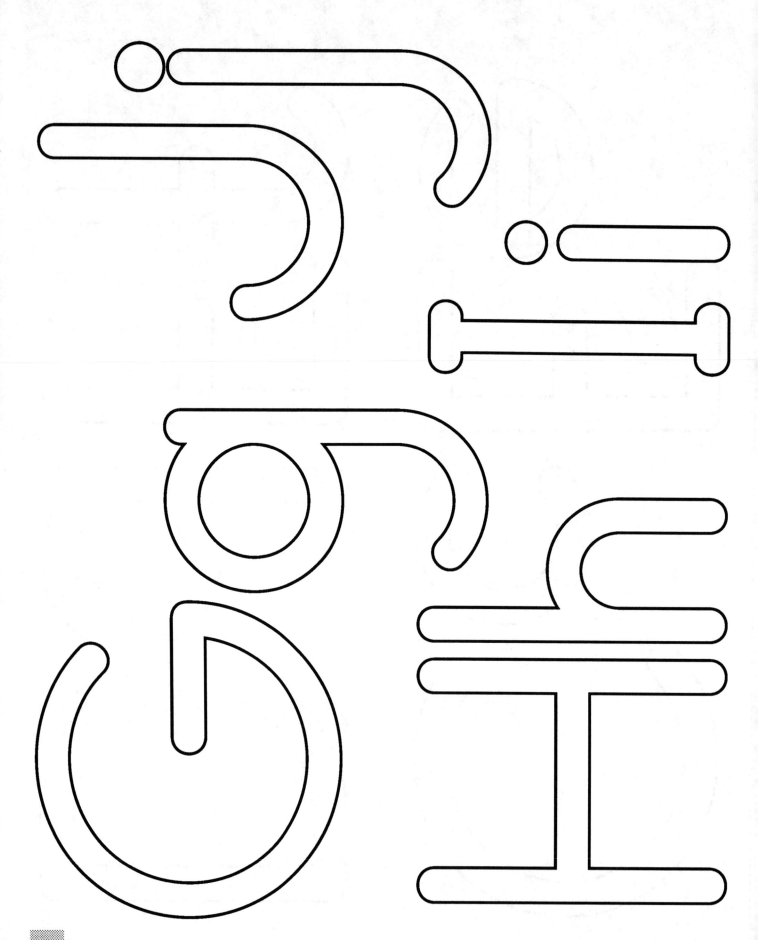

Alphabet Pocket Fun

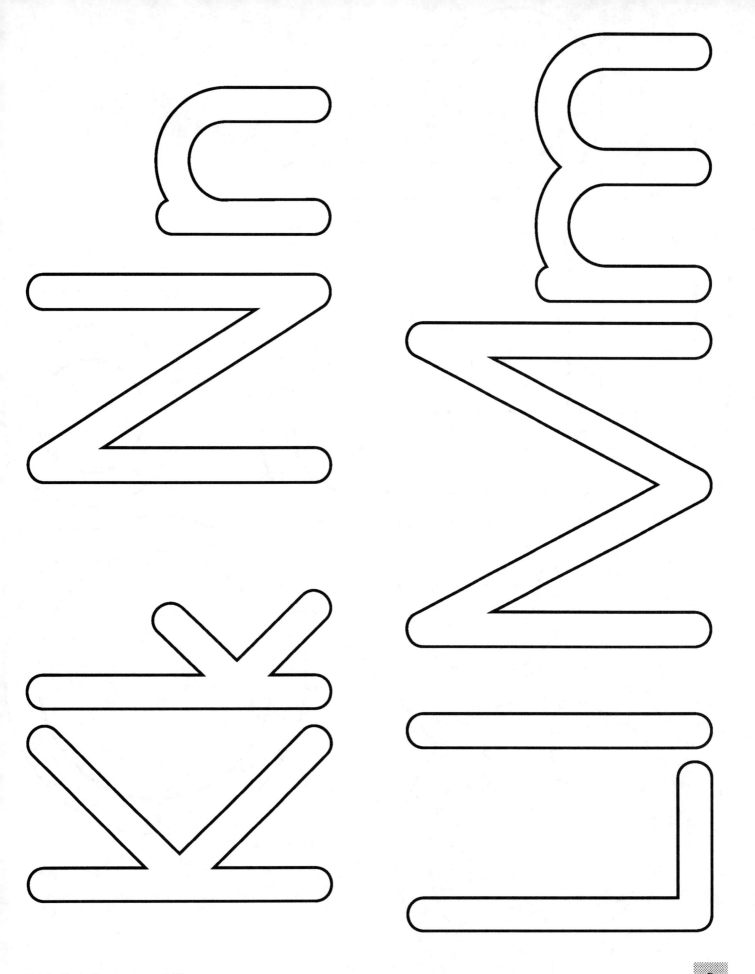

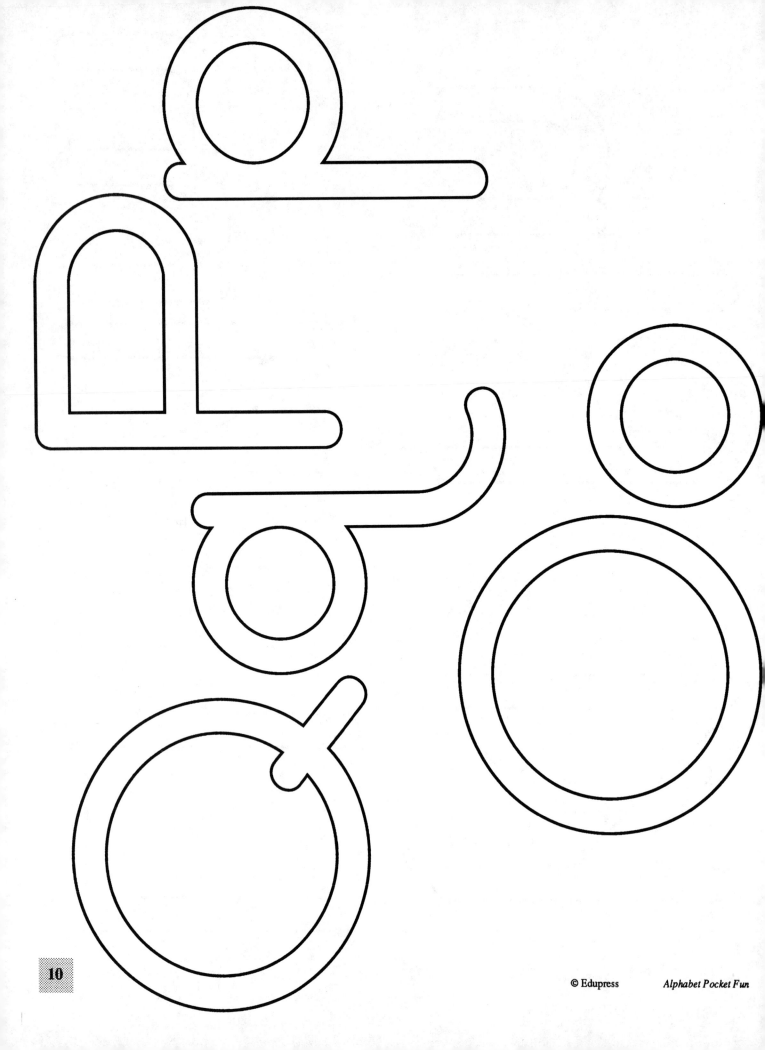

Alphabet Pocket Fun

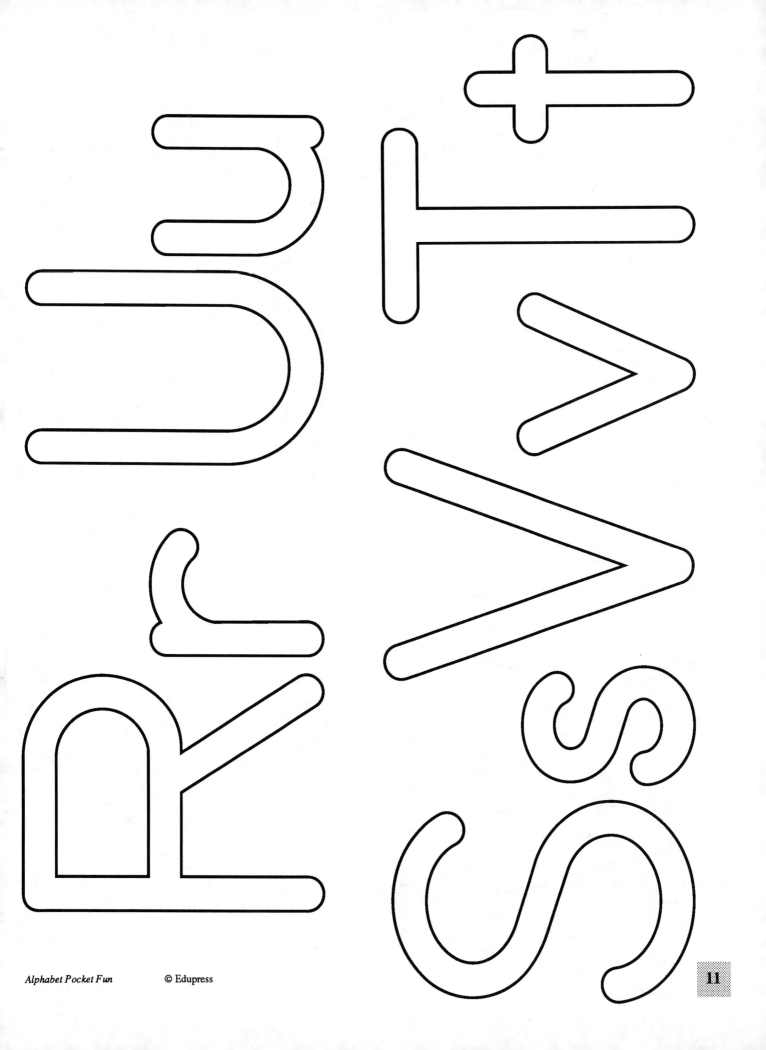

Alphabet Pocket Fun

ape

ant

apron

apple

Alphabet Pocket Fun

B

bell

bird

bucket

boat

Alphabet Pocket Fun

C

cow

cat

cup

car

Alphabet Pocket Fun

D

dinosaur

doll

dog

duck

Alphabet Pocket Fun

E

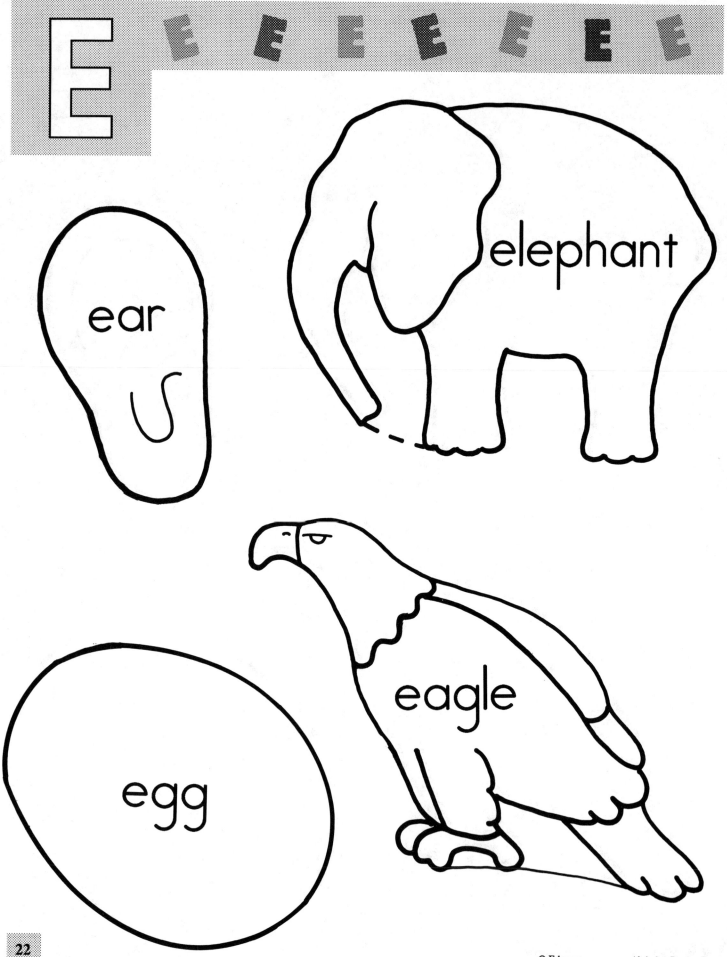

ear

elephant

egg

eagle

© Edupress   *Alphabet Pocket Fun*

F

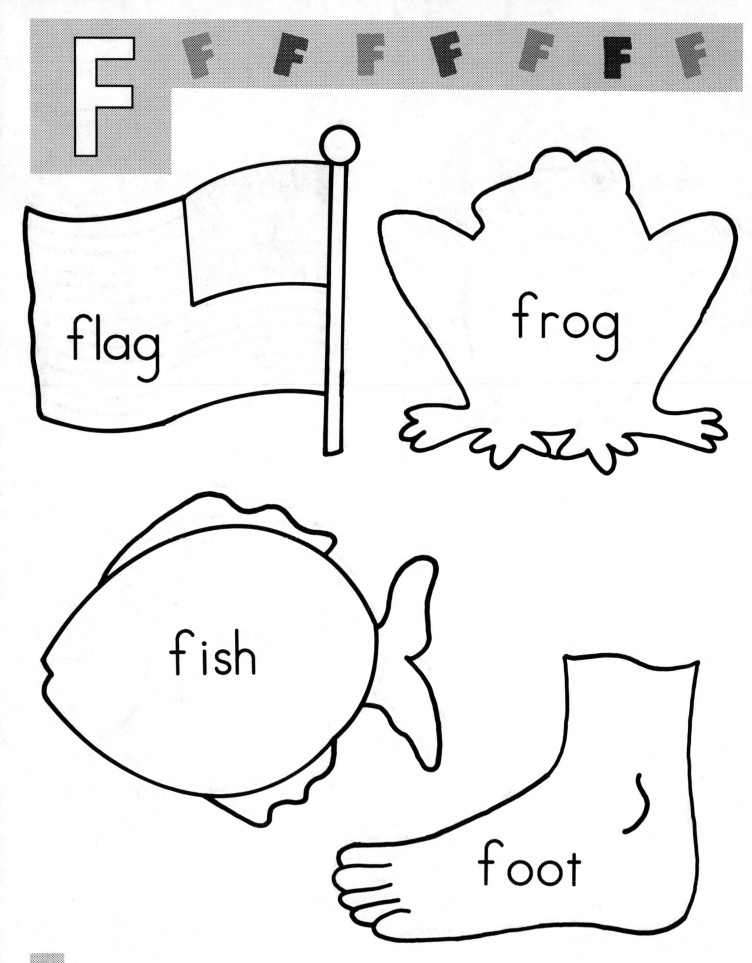

flag

frog

fish

foot

Alphabet Pocket Fun

G

G

grapes

glasses

giant

giraffe

Alphabet Pocket Fun

H

horse

heart

hat

hippo

28

Alphabet Pocket Fun

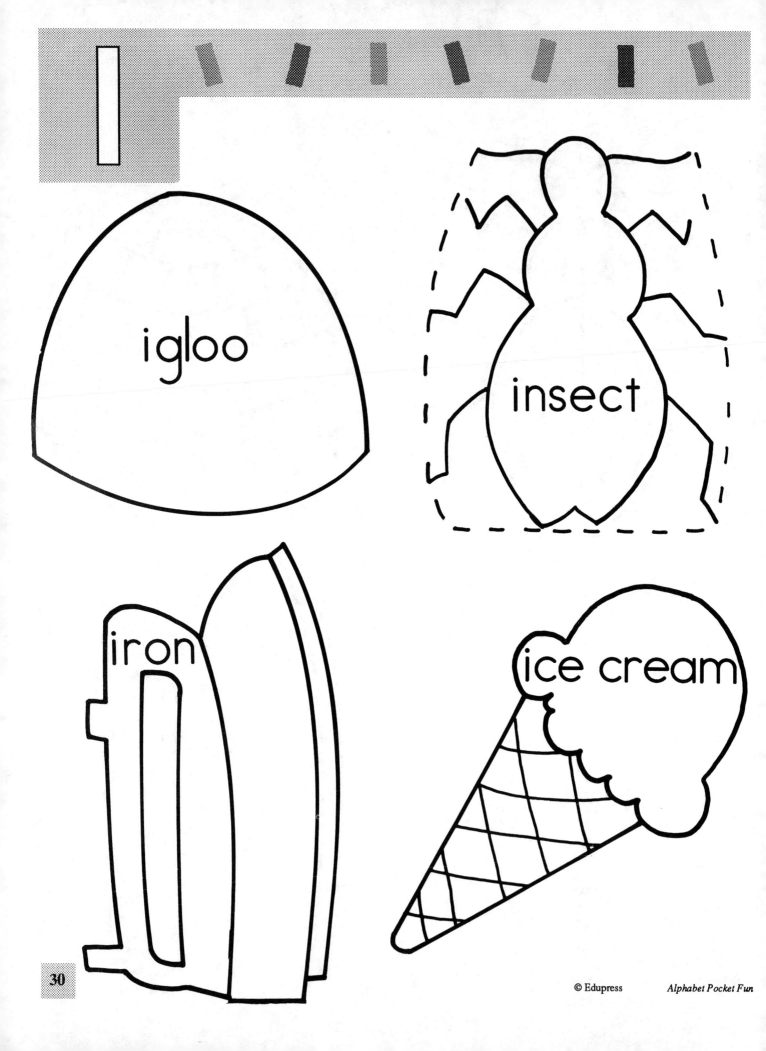

igloo

insect

iron

ice cream

Alphabet Pocket Fun

jacket

jeans

jar

jet

Alphabet Pocket Fun

K

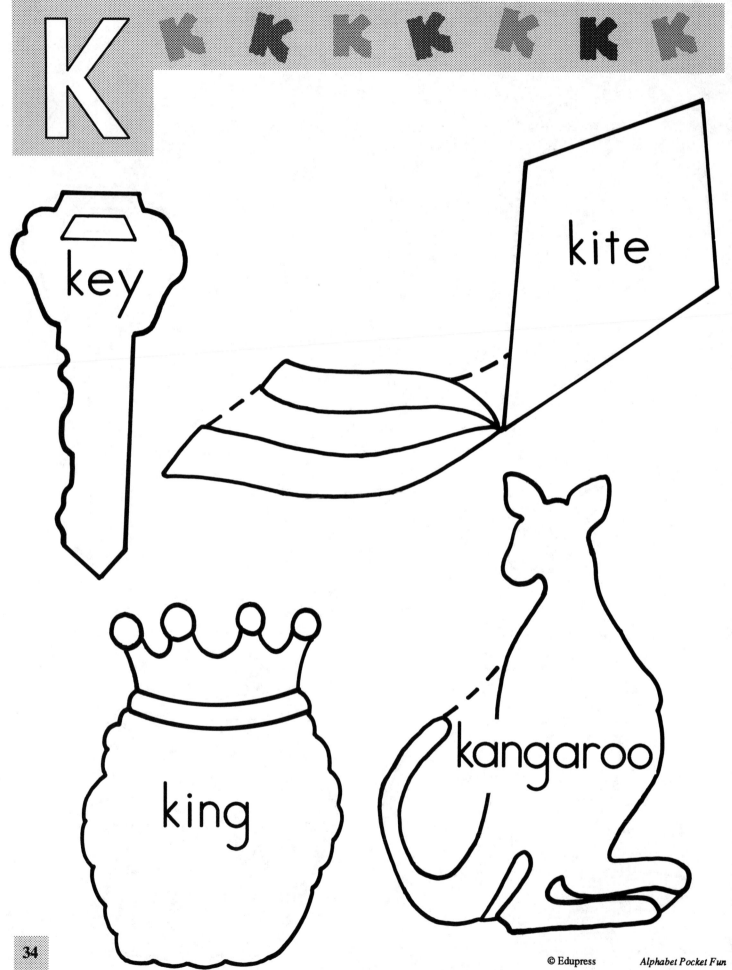

key

kite

king

kangaroo

Alphabet Pocket Fun

lemon

leaf

ladybug

log

Alphabet Pocket Fun

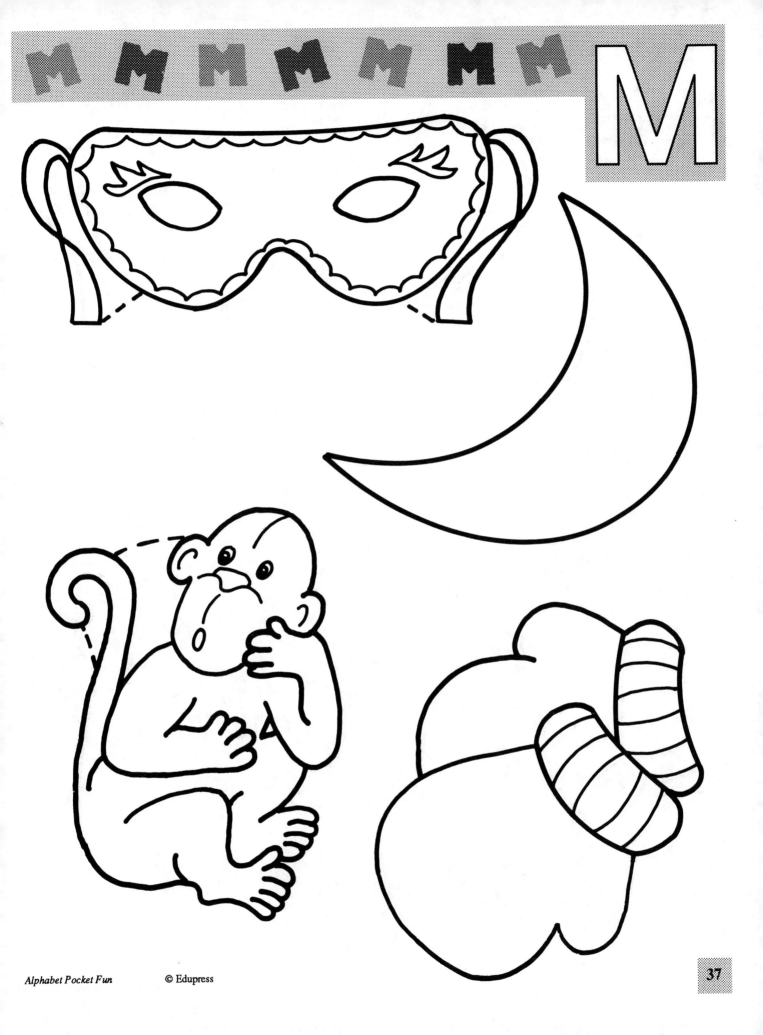

M

mask

moon

mittens

monkey

Alphabet Pocket Fun

DAILY WORLD

WHAT HAPPENED

N

DAILY WORLD

news

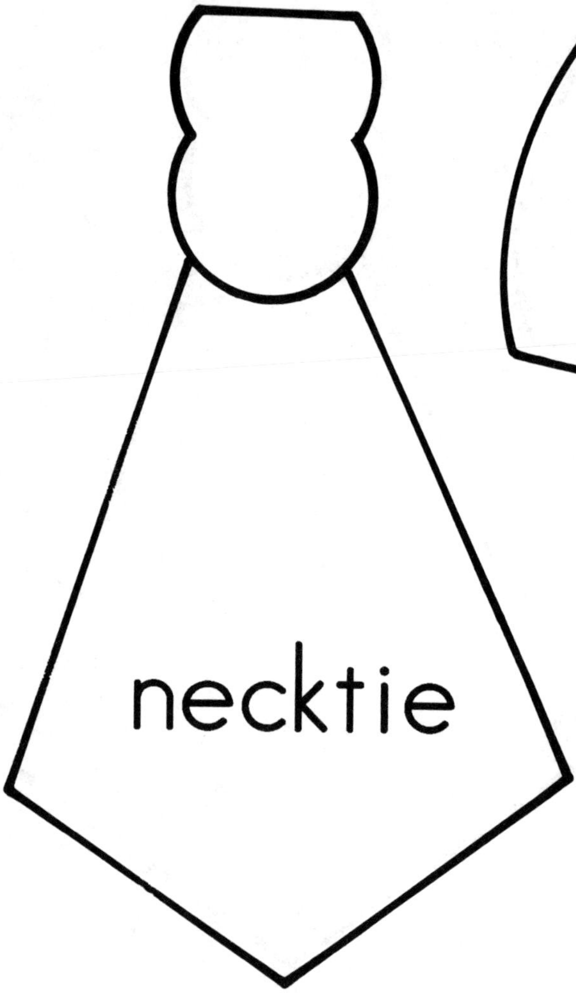

necktie

nest

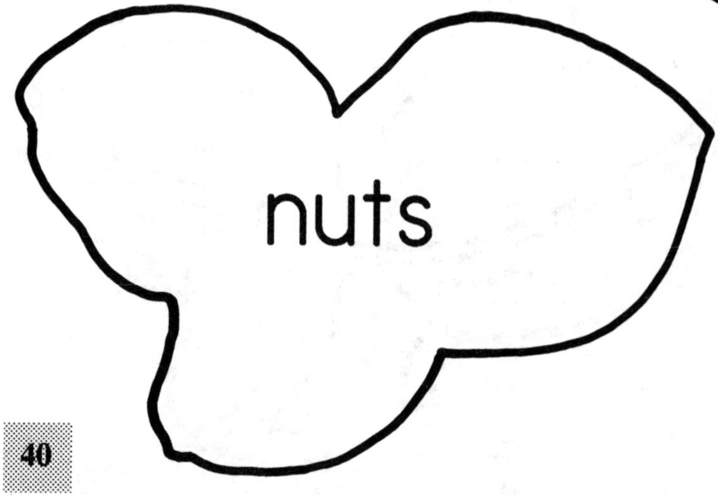

nuts

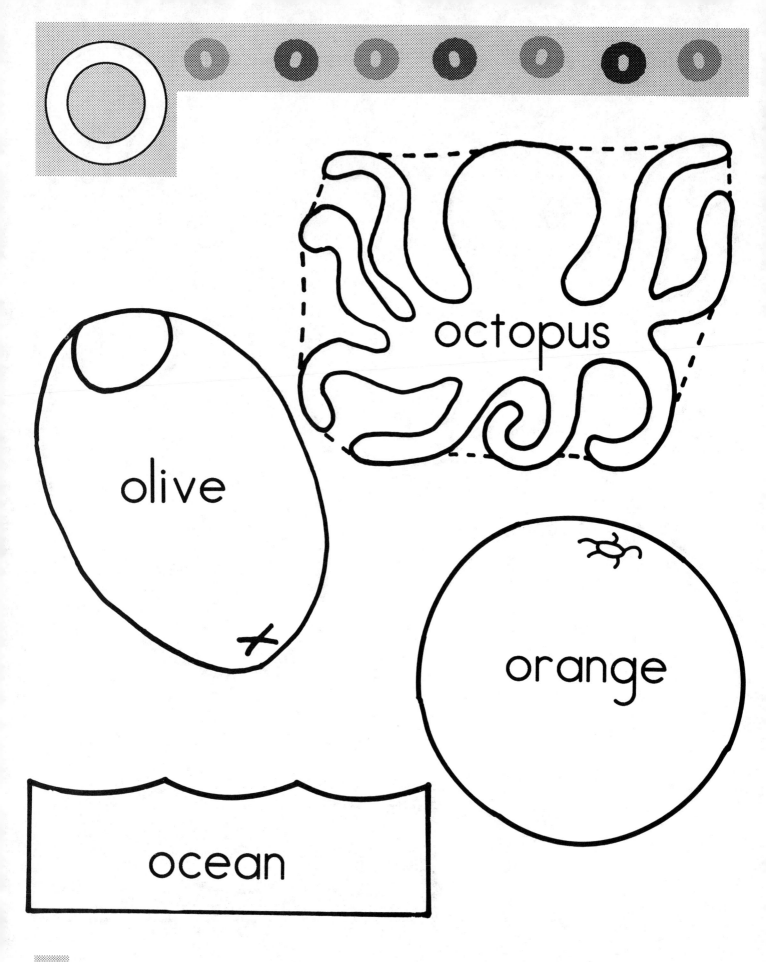

octopus

olive

orange

ocean

Alphabet Pocket Fun

pencil

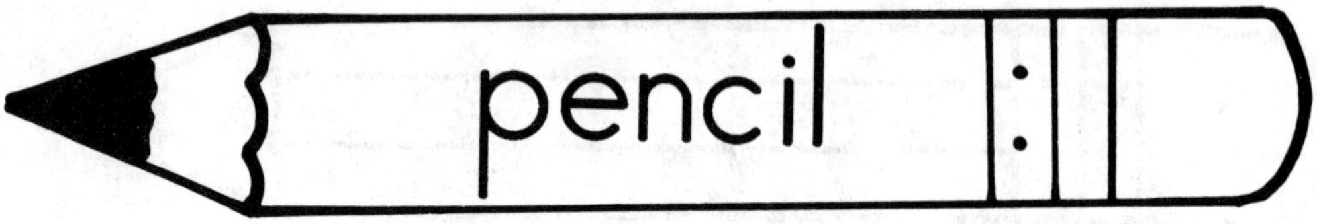

pig

pie

plane

© Edupress   *Alphabet Pocket Fun*

question

queen

quilt

quail

Alphabet Pocket Fun

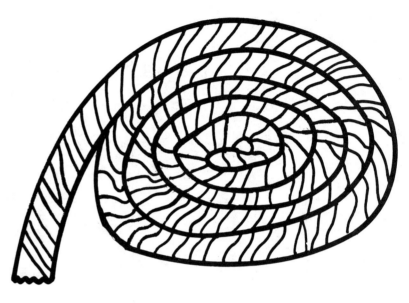

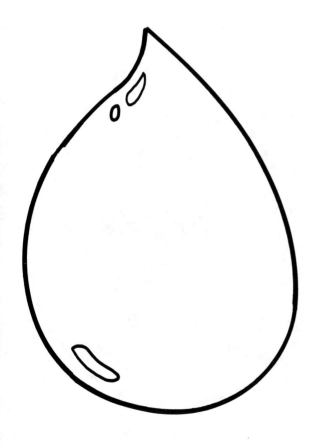

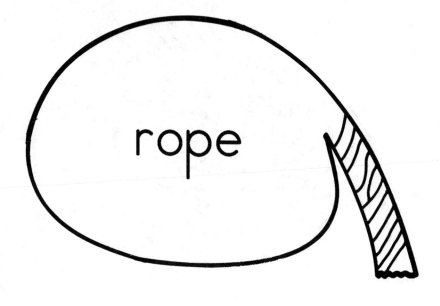

rope

ring

rabbit

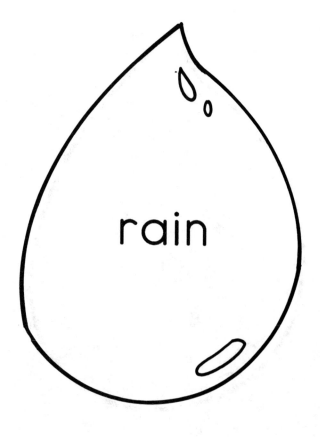

rain

Alphabet Pocket Fun

S

snail

sun

sock

star

© Edupress *Alphabet Pocket Fun*

T

truck

train

telephone

turtle

Alphabet Pocket Fun

United States

upstairs

umbrella

unicorn

© Edupress   *Alphabet Pocket Fun*

V

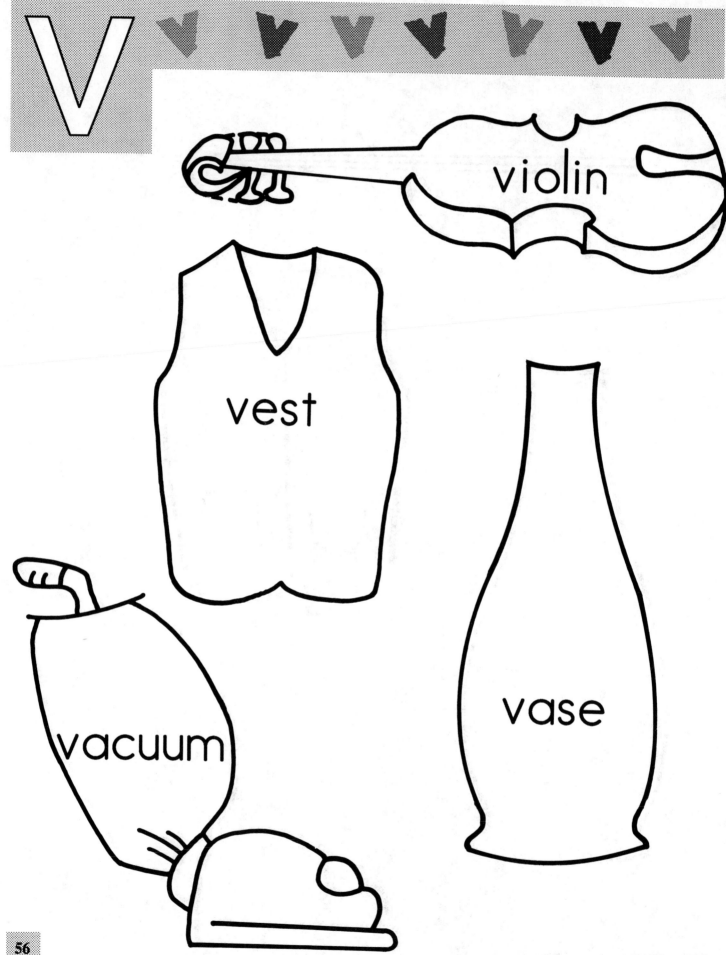

violin

vest

vase

vacuum

Alphabet Pocket Fun

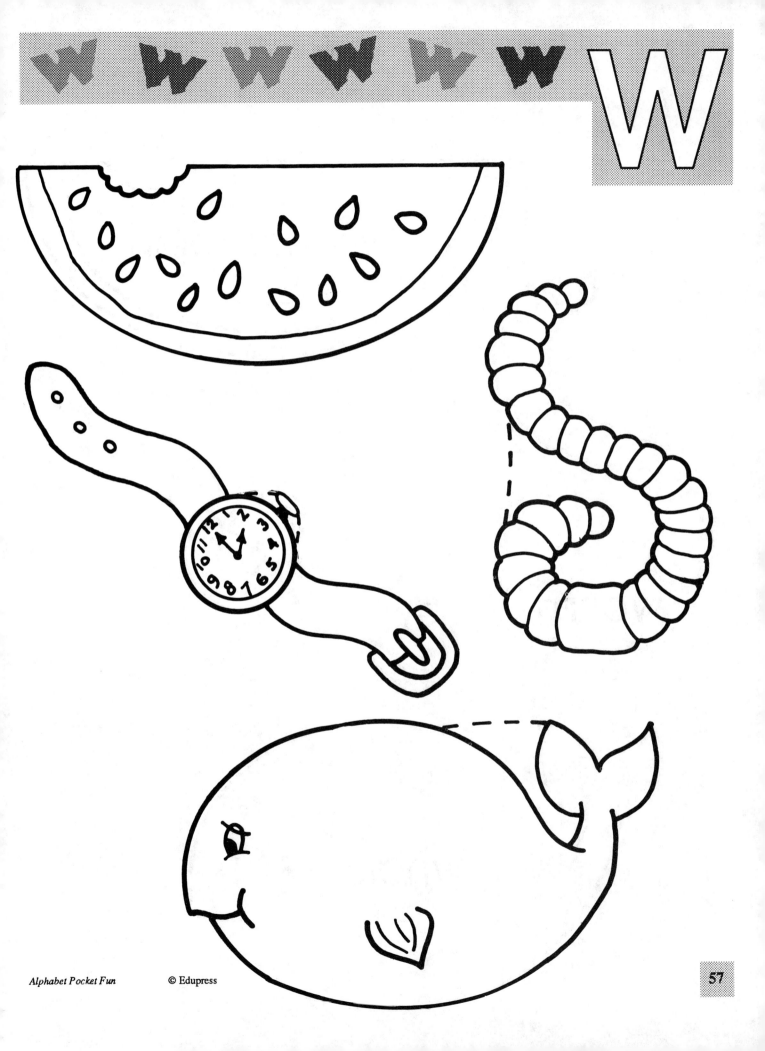

W

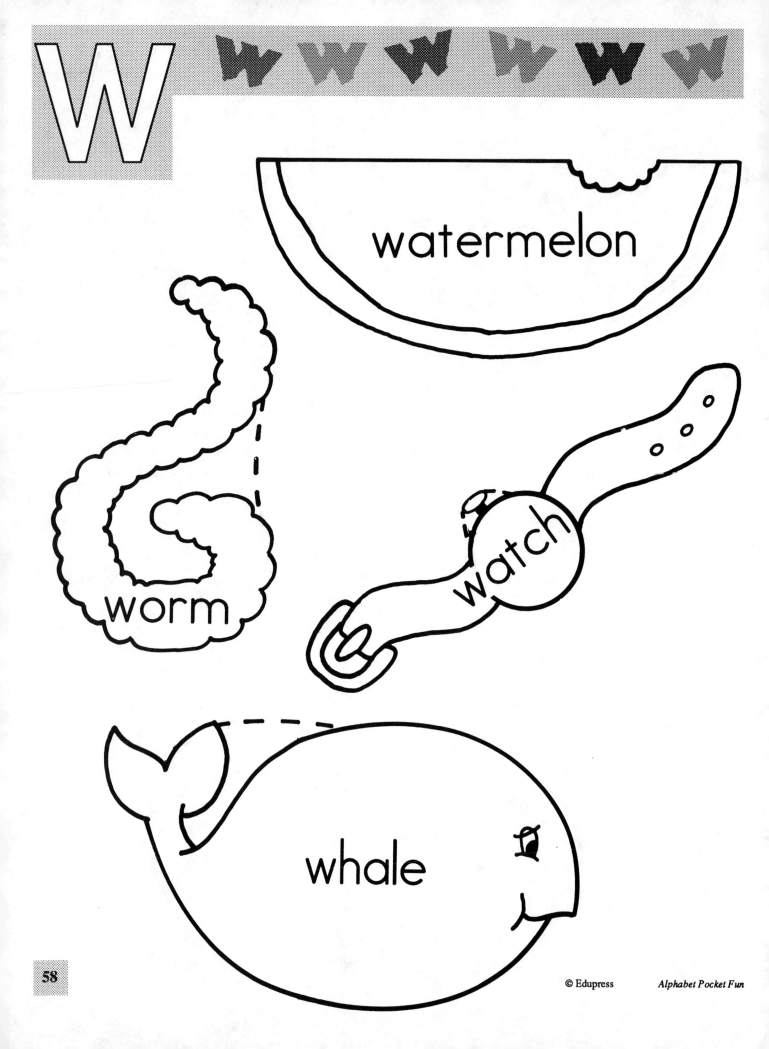

watermelon

worm

watch

whale

Alphabet Pocket Fun

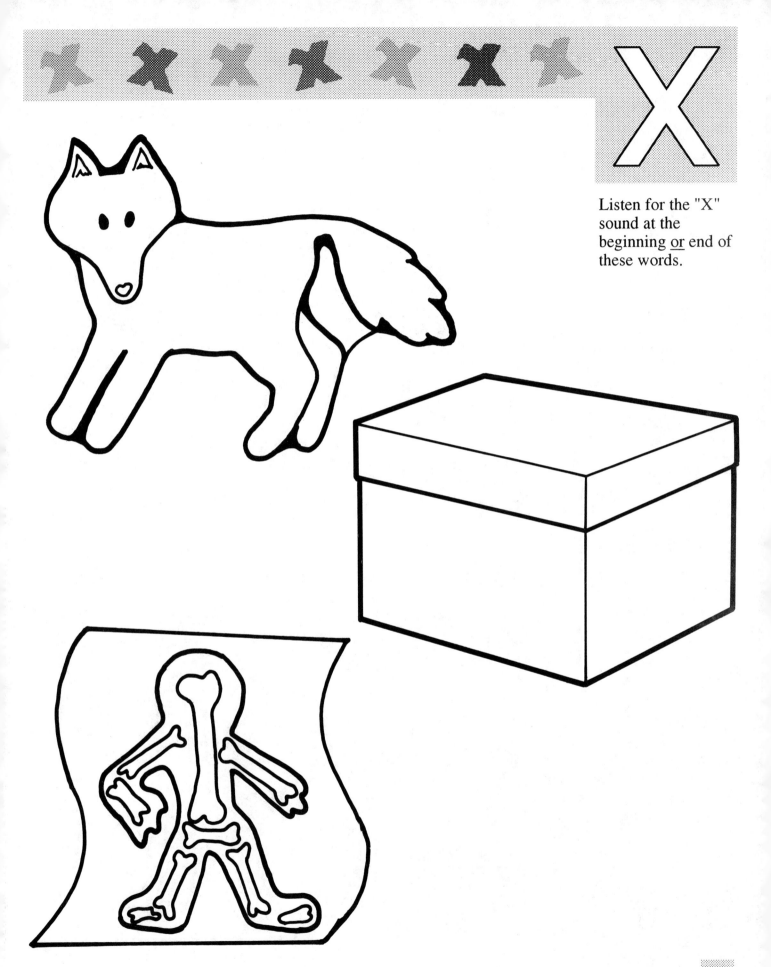

X

Listen for the "X" sound at the beginning or end of these words.

X

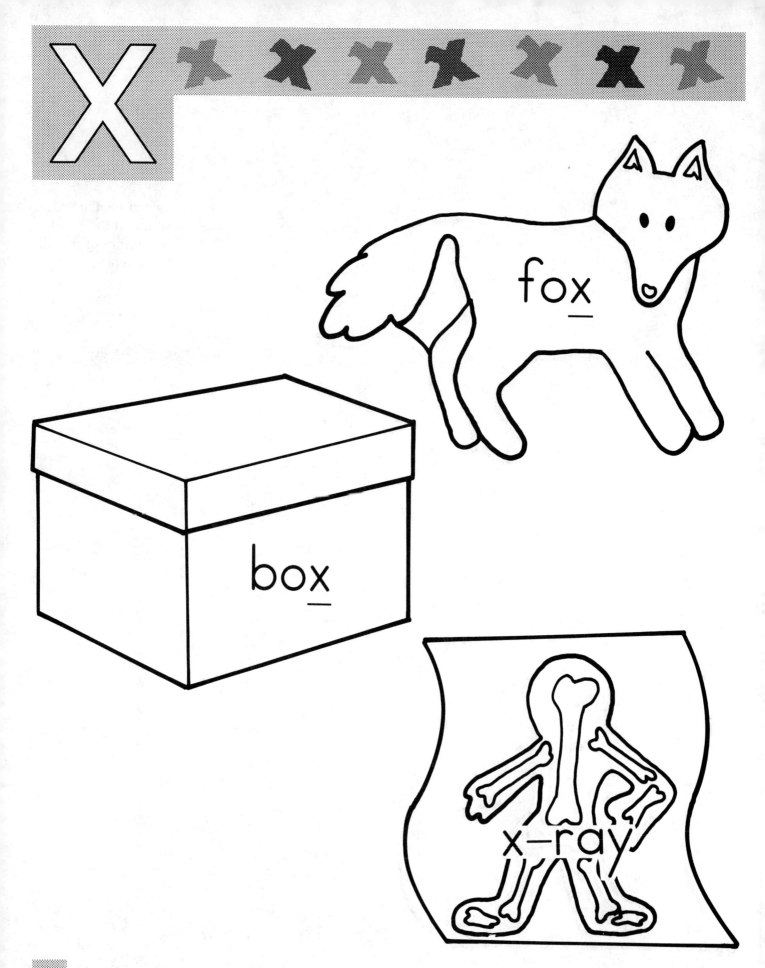

fox

box

x-ray

Alphabet Pocket Fun

Y

yarn

yacht

yo-yo

yam

© Edupress   *Alphabet Pocket Fun*

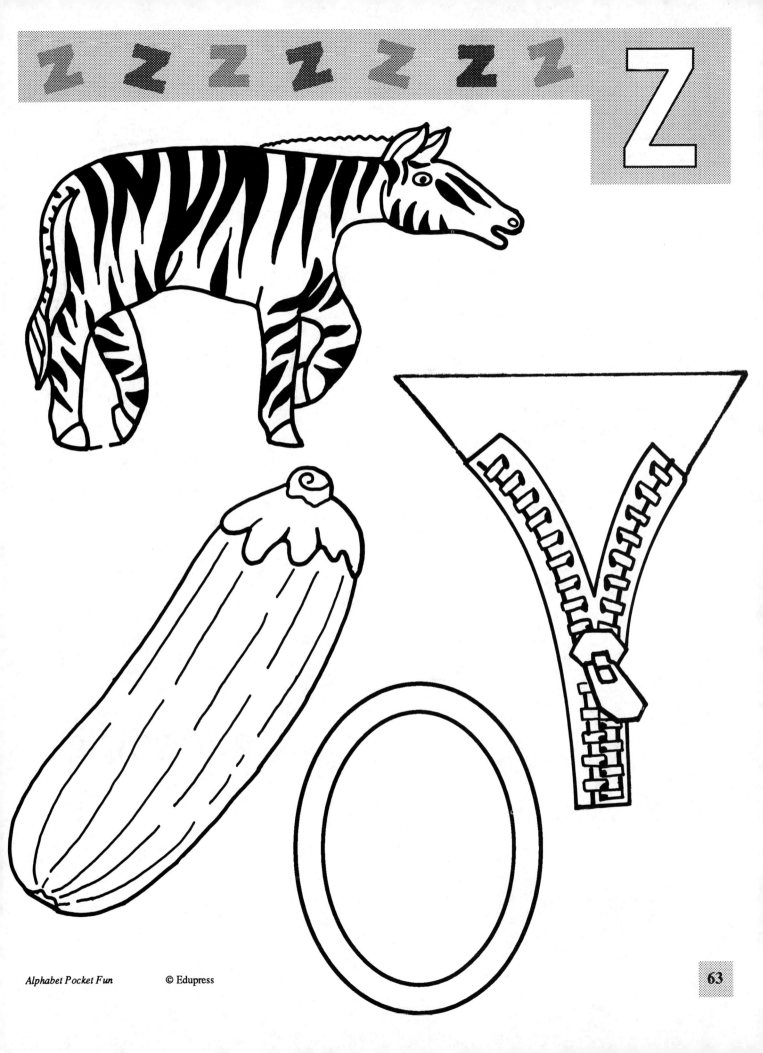

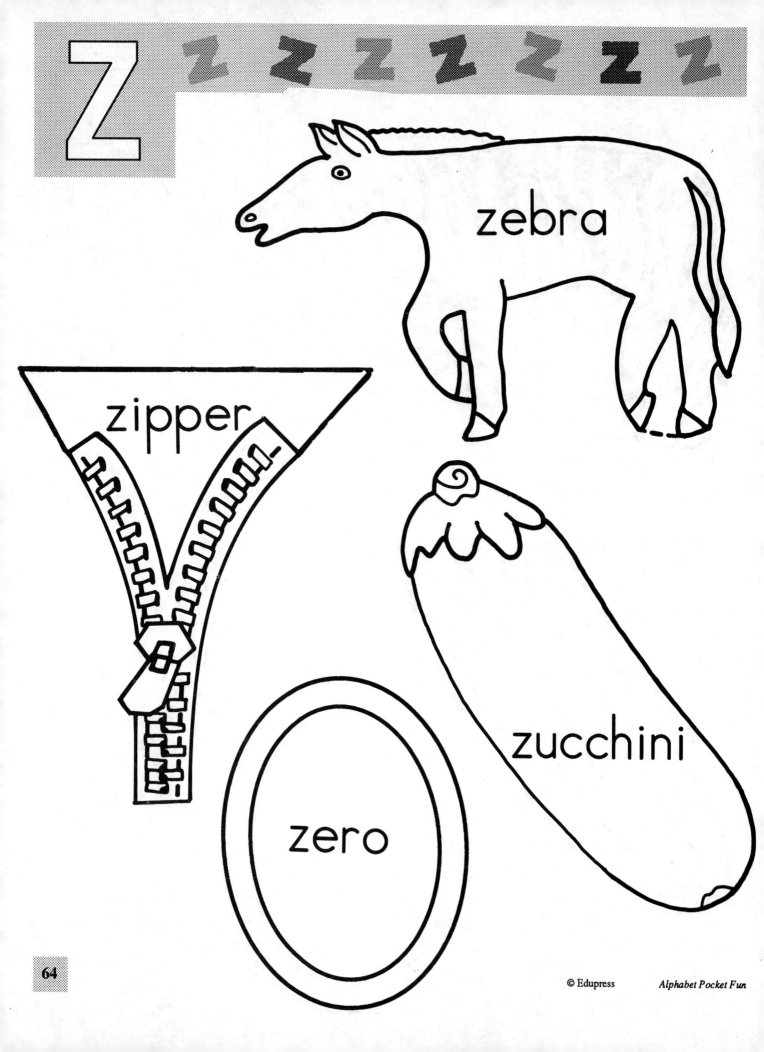

Z z z z z z z z z

zebra

zipper

zucchini

zero

64

© Edupress   *Alphabet Pocket Fun*